MARGARET MONDRAGON

A Tribute to a Mother I Grew to Love

How looking past hurt helps us see qualities we can love

This book was professionally typeset on Reedsy.
Find out more at reedsy.com

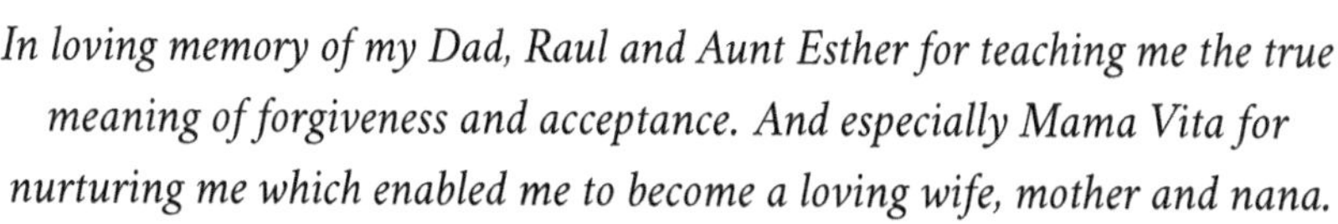

In loving memory of my Dad, Raul and Aunt Esther for teaching me the true meaning of forgiveness and acceptance. And especially Mama Vita for nurturing me which enabled me to become a loving wife, mother and nana.

I'm dedicating this book to my husband, Richard, our daughters, Monica and Amanda and our five grandchildren, Andrew, Gage, Gianna, Zander and Giovanni. Thank you all for your never ending love!

Contents

One

Introduction

This is the true story and a tribute to my mom, who I grew to love. We were fortunate to have her live with me and my husband, Richard, along with my brother, Rick.

The truth is, when I was growing up, we did not have a great relationship. In fact, it was very rocky when I lived at home with her and my four brothers. So much so that I married my high school sweetheart at the early age of seventeen, just to get out of the house. However, I made a conscious decision to look past the abuse of my childhood and focus on how to break that cycle so that I could raise a loving family...and forgive my mother and brothers. Thanks to this positive mindset and my ability to forgive and love those around me, Richard and I have two beautiful and loving daughters and five grandchildren, who are just as loving. We are truly blessed.

When my mom was 99 years young, she needed a new place to live, and we were not about to let her go to a facility. Fortunately, we had a new home where she was welcomed to live with us. This is our story.

Two

Back Story

My grandparents were born in the mid-1800's. My grandmother already had ten children by the time she became pregnant with my mom. My grandmother thought she was done having children, but to her surprise, she became pregnant once again with my mom who was born at the end of 1919. She was the 11th child of twelve children. My grandmother had started all her daughters' names with an "E." But, when mom was born, my grandmother thought for sure she was the last, so she named my mother after herself, "Otilia." That was common in those years because they had such large families. Not much originality back then. Mother's nickname became "Tillie" and she was, as we say in Spanish, "la preferida", the preferred one. All her siblings and parents doted on her, even after her baby sister was born, who did end up with an "E" name.

Tillie in her 30's and after she married my Dad

Fast forward a few decades. Tillie married late in life for her generation, as it was uncommon for an adult to marry in their 30's. I never did find out why she waited to get married. That is a secret she took to the grave. Regardless, she married my dad, who was in the Army, and proceeded to have children. I was the only daughter and became his "little princess," which my mother did not care for. Remember, she was la preferida and was not used to competition. She always expected to be the center of attention. Sadly, she was not happy being a military spouse, because she did not like living away from her family, especially her mom. So, they split up in 1961, after she had my youngest brother.

Being a single parent of five children was not easy during the 60's and 70's, but she did the best she could. I am sure some of you have heard the term, "It takes a village to raise children," and she had the help of two of her sisters, who were spinsters. "Spinster" is a term used back then for women who never married. I considered them my bonus grandmothers because they were much older than my mom. They taught me how to cook, bake, sew, knit, and crochet. I was extremely fortunate to have them in my life.

Tillie was fortunate to retire at 61 years of age and she thoroughly enjoyed her free time. She was able to go and come whenever and wherever she pleased, without having to punch a time clock, which she used to her advantage to do the things loved. She especially enjoyed being a grandmother to our girls and seeing her friends and family.

Early in her retirement, mom's favorite pastime was fishing. She was not simply good at it, she excelled at it- like a pro. Before retiring and when we were kids, she would take us fishing and crabbing. That was fun for us as youngsters, not so much when we got older. Anyway, she went fishing every day before the crack of dawn, with or without a fishing buddy. She would even take our daughters fishing with her every chance she had, and they enjoyed it just as much. She truly lived for fishing. And I am not talking about sitting on a bench on some pier for a brief period. I am talking about hard core fishing for hours on end. She would go surf-fishing in the inter coastal canal or at Padre Island National Seashore. Depending on the day, you could find her there or on the jetties near Mustang Island or near Corpus Christi University (today it is called Texas A&M Corpus Christi). If anyone invited her to go fishing on a boat, she would jump at the opportunity. She never turned down an invitation to go fishing.

Mom with Andrew

After we moved our family to San Antonio, mom struggled to maintain her big house and yard. So, one day she called me and announced that she was selling her house and was moving in with us. Not exactly my ideal scenario, given our rocky past, she just said she was doing it. I was not about to argue with her, because I was afraid of her. Regardless, she lived with us for several years and it was great having her. Especially because she got to enjoy our first grandson, Andrew, her first great-grandchild. She would spend time riding him up and down the street in his little wagon. That all ended after my dad's wife passed away though. He wanted to be near us, so I invited him to stay with us in one of the other spare bedrooms. When I told mom that dad was moving in, she was livid and cussed me out in front of Richard. How dare I choose him over her. Remember, she had to be the center of attention. She moved out shortly thereafter. I was confused…prior to that, when dad would visit us, he would stay a few days and mom would make him coffee and cook or bake for him, so to me, they seemed to get along fine. Obviously, I was wrong.

Over the next few years, she lived with some of my other brothers and finally settled in with my oldest brother outside of Houston. He was single and had a large two-story house. It was just the two of them, so everything was sunshine and rainbows and then things started spiraling downward. When mom was 93 years old, her driving became questionable, so we all decided it was time for her to stop driving. She was pretty upset about that, but we could not blame her. She was used to her independence. Then over the years, she was hospitalized frequently, until my brother could not take care of her.

Three

Early 2019 – The Invitation and Move

◦◦◦

Mother's health progressively deteriorated over the next few years with some falls and frequently ended up in the hospital with a UTI (urinary tract infection). It got to the point that my older brother could not always be home to take care of her. So, we had to look at other options. One brother wanted to take her with him to Dallas, but she refused to go with him. As I mentioned earlier, we were not about to have her live in a facility with strangers and not in a place where we could not visit her frequently. We wanted her close by.

Eventually, my brother, Rick, offered to take her in and it was settled that she would go back to Corpus Christi. Unfortunately, unbeknownst to us, Rick's house was severely damaged by hurricane Harvey, and it became unlivable. Without hesitation, Richard and I invited mom and Rick to move into our home. It was a newly built one-story house, with two spare bedrooms and an open floor plan with wide doorways to accommodate her wheelchair or walker. Our other brothers were not keen on the idea, but they had to give in, because there was no other place for her to go, or that she was willing to go. Originally, it was supposed to be for a few months and then she would go between our house and my brother near Dallas, but she wanted to stay with us permanently. We were fine with that…whatever she wanted, just to make her happy.

In early April, mom and Rick finally moved in with us. The excitement of them coming was electrifying. Because prior to this, me and my family were not always welcome to visit mother at my brother's house. So, to have her with us was a blessing and allowed us to make up for lost time. We excitedly prepared for her arrival by buying all sorts of things we anticipated she would need or want. We had so many things planned, and the future was looking bright. We could not wait to spoil and love on her, and our grand-kids were ecstatic about her moving in with us, because they could visit her whenever they wanted.

Rick and mom's rooms were across a short hall, with a bathroom in between their rooms. He was her main caregiver and I helped when I could, since I was still working a full-time job, as was Richard. Our oldest daughter, Monica, would visit and help with mom. She was a former CNA (Certified Nurse's Aide), so she was extremely knowledgeable about taking care of seniors. Mom loved having her around and they could talk about flowers and plants, because that is what they had in common. When our youngest daughter, Amanda, visited, she would spoil mother rotten and mom loved it. The laughter from their conversations was contagious. It was a remarkable sight, and I never tired of the sound.

Amanda with Grandma Tillie

After mom arrived, the reality of her inability to do things for herself was unexpected. We had seen her in December, the prior year and did not realize how frail she had become over the past several months. She lost a lot of weight, and we were told that she was not eating well. I could not help but wonder if they had sent her here to die. What a terrible thought. I could not believe the difference in her appearance from the last time we saw her. I certainly did not expect it.

Mom as she sharpens the knives

Rick and I were determined to get her healthy and independent again.

Rick prepared most of her meals to include veggies, a starch, and a good protein. She started to eat better with each passing day. We gradually started to have her do things by herself. We would help her, but we wanted her to realize that she was still very capable of doing things without assistance. Over time, she started walking better with her walker, getting dressed, going to the potty, serving her own coffee and other trivial things. I even had her sharpen all the knives in the house. She was phenomenal at it and aside from her strength, her memory was as sharp as a tack , better than a lot of people I know.

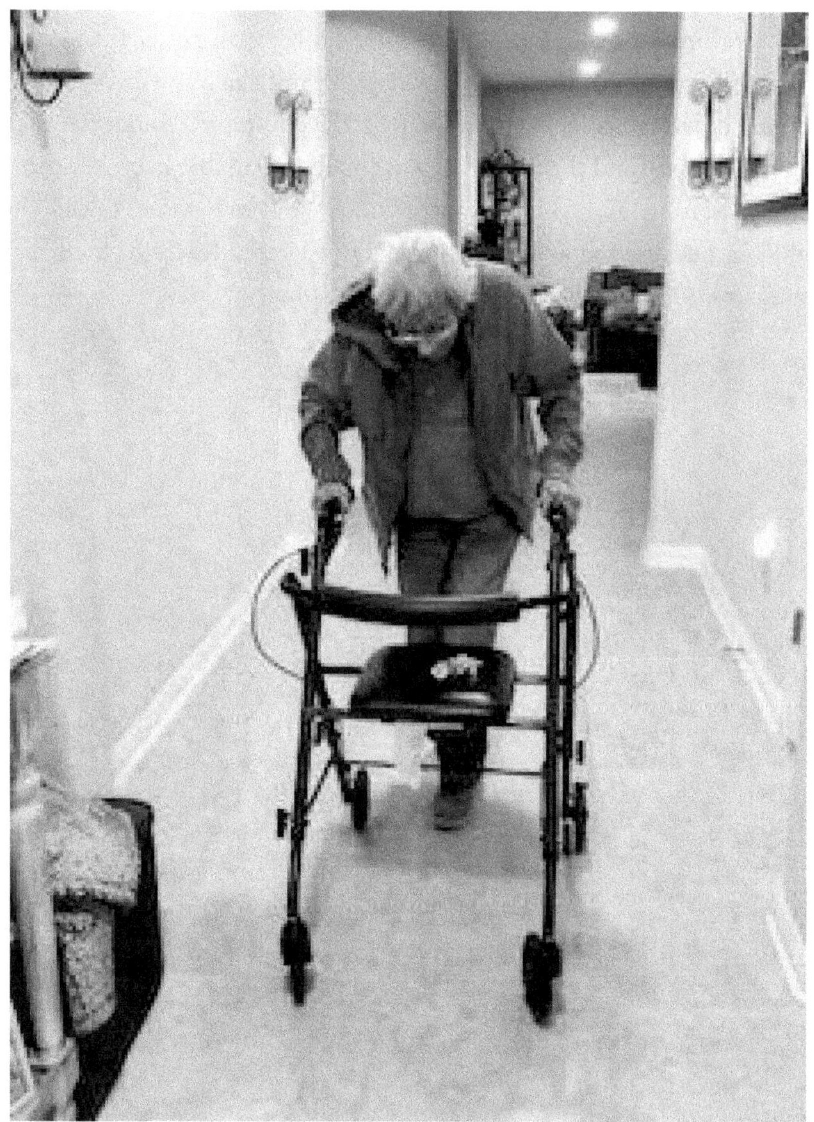

Mom getting around the house on her own

Over time, her eating habits improved and so did her health, thanks to Rick. Her doctor was even impressed with her weight gain, not to mention, her overall health. Her blood-work was better than most young people. Not once did she have a UTI while she was with us. Aside from her weight gain, her personality started to return to normal and she was happy and thriving. She was finally doing things on her own and we started taking her out of the house, we even took her to church with us, because she would enjoy watching Monica teach in children's ministry. All in all, mom was finally flourishing.

Taking Mom to Church

Four

Her Colorful Personality

Tillie had so many friends of all ages and they all adored her, as did all our family members. If you are wondering why, plainly put, it was her colorful personality. You see, she was a true figment of our imagination. She was a woman ahead of her own time! She loved loud colors. No matter where she went or the occasion, she always dressed to the nines and always in bright, beautiful colors and prints. When she attended someone's funeral, she never dressed in black. She wanted to let everyone know that she appreciated the person who passed and wanted to celebrate their life with color, and she wore them loud and proud.

Mother was a friend to anyone in need and always had an open-door policy at home, for friends or family. Whenever somebody was sick, she would cook some soup to take to them and she would tell us, "I've gotta take care of the old people," as she referred to anyone who was usually more than 20 years younger than she was. Whenever Rick had a sailing event in Corpus, mom would open her home to anyone who needed a place to stay. I am not talking about two or three people either. She would have blankets and sleeping bags all over her floors to accommodate up to twenty people and fed every single one of them. She truly had a servant's heart. She served others with her love and simple presence.

Grandma hugging Gio

Mother would light up a room as she made her grand entrance, and everyone (I mean EVERYBODY) wanted to get a hug from her. She would hug you like she had not seen you in years, long and strong. That is not an exaggeration at all. When she hugged you, you could hear your back pop. Yes, she was one strong cookie. Her hugs were filled with so much love, it would penetrate your soul. Anyone who knew her, would tell you they loved her hugs. Nobody came close to her with those hugs, except for our two older grandsons, Andrew, and Gage. But I miss her hugs the most.

Goldie and Mom

When mom was invited to a party, she would tell them, "I'll be there with bells on!" She would say that all the time. But she truly was a party animal. She was the belle of the ball, even if it was somebody's birthday, graduation, wedding or whatever the occasion. Ricky took her to her best friend's birthday party in San Marcos in 2019. As she entered the room, everyone shouted, "Tillie's here!" and mom had a blast.

Mom kicking up her heels at a dance, with a little help from Lettie and I

Mom loved dancing. Whenever she was invited to a dance of any sort, she was on the dance floor. Her love of dancing was evident when people of all ages asked her to dance. She never refused an offer. She told me that a good dancer is someone who could follow and make them look good, no matter how bad they danced. I too love dancing and realized that I am just like her in that respect.

Mother was so funny and quick-witted, but I do not believe she thought so. Honestly, she could not tell a joke to save her soul, but the things she said and how she said them, plus her timing, was impeccable. She had a way of lightening a mood with her play on words. One time, when the girls were young and we were traveling near Austin, mom saw a sign for Bastrop, TX. Suddenly, she yelled, "Look girls, we're passing Bastard, TX!" I was shocked but, at the same time, it was hilarious. You see, we had been on the road for over an hour, and it was quiet and a bit boring, so she felt that she needed to lighten the mood to make us laugh and boy, did we. All of us laughed for quite a while after that, and then the girls kept asking mom, "Where are we now?" All the while, I am looking at her, just waiting for the next zinger to come out of her mouth. In fact, I am giggling as I write this, because that was so her. She was unexpectedly funny.

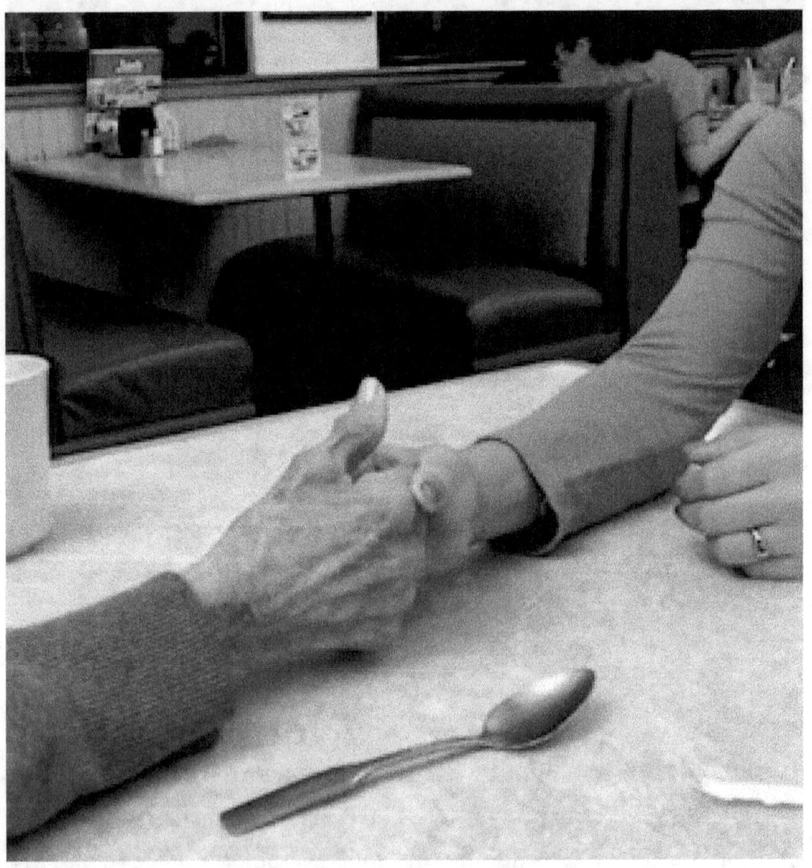

Gigi and Mom playing thumb wars

Mom was notorious for cheating at games with anyone and everyone. My granddaughter, Gigi, taught her how to play thumb wars and mom cheated every single time. Gigi would tell her, "Grandma, you're cheating!" she would cover her mouth laughing and rub her hands. What a sight! My cousins came to visit her and brought their loteria game (that is a Mexican game of bingo) and she cheated at that, too. Mom had no shame in her game and did not care if she got caught. All we could do was laugh. Of course, we had always let her win. How could we not? That lady was so freaking funny, and we did not care if she cheated. We enjoyed watching her win…every single time.

Mom loved jazz music to her core. In fact, she was one of the founding members of Corpus Christi's Texas Jazz Festival. She attended every annual event, right up until 2019. Rick took mom to the festival, a couple of months prior to her 100th birthday. She enjoyed every minute of it and got to see so many people. She drank her cold beer and was taken to the dance floor so she could dance in her wheelchair, laughing and soaking it up. People could not believe she was there. She told them, "Hell, I wouldn't miss it for the world!"

Mom also had a green thumb, just like Mother Nature, herself. She could plant and grow ANYTHING! If I had a plant, it would die in no time, regardless of how hard I took care of it. Her, on the other hand, could grow anything. I witnessed her eating an orange one day and she spit out the seeds from her mouth and planted them in a planter next to her on the patio. Those seeds took like crazy and quickly grew into three thriving orange tree saplings. I wanted them to have a chance to grow, so I gave two of the saplings to Rick and one to Monica. They have green thumbs just like mom.

Mom with her baseball team

Mom was a major sports buff, primarily baseball and football, with baseball being her favorite. If a game were on TV, we could not bother her for a second, especially if the Houston Astros were playing. She could tell you the stats of every player and not just for the Astros, any team. To top that off, she knew about their personal lives. I honestly do not know how she knew so much. In fact, while in her twenties, she played baseball during WWII, while the men were at war. And I understood that as a lefty, she was a great shortstop, and she wrote with her right hand. Ironically, I too write with my right, but throw with my left. Football was her second favorite sport, and her favorite team was the Dallas Cowboys. She was not into all the drama with the players, except for a select few, but she knew the team's history and their record better than the average Joe.

Mother had the vocabulary of a sailor. Anyone who knew her well could tell you that she could make a sailor blush. It came out more while she watched baseball. When the Astros would mess up or the other team scored, she would get so excited, that the swearing was often loud. My grand-kids loved watching her and would laugh at her when she swore, then they would go give her a tight hug, to let her know they loved her just the way she was. She would swear like it was nobody's business. I loved that about her.

If anyone asked her why she had lived so long she would pick up her right hand, folding in her three middle fingers, while sticking out her thumb and pinkie, as if drinking a glass of beer, her favorite alcoholic beverage. In fact, we asked her doctor if it was okay for her to have her alcohol and he said, "At her age, she can have anything she pleases!" Mom loved hearing that. She enjoyed a small can of beer for lunch and a shot glass of a sweet liqueur in the evenings. As soon as she heard my husband walk into the house every evening, she would yell, "Hey, Mr. Richard, I'll drink to that!" That was his cue to serve her a shot glass of her liqueur. Her favorite was "Tres Leches," and we would drive all over town looking for it, until they stopped making it. She was so upset about that. When

we finally ran out, we had to hunt for another type of liqueur and it was not easy, but we would do anything to make that lady happy

Five

Reconnecting and Rebuilding Relationships

As I mentioned earlier, mom and I had a very rocky relationship when I was living at home. Our mother and daughter relationship did not flourish until after I got married and had my girls. You see, I learned that forgiveness allows love to flow in all relationships and ours only grew greater with time. I never asked her why she treated me the way she did, when I was younger, because I did not care, and as far as I was concerned, that was a lifetime ago. I moved on and became a better person for it. That allowed me to love her with every passing day.

My husband, Richard, was her "favorite" son-in-law. Honestly, he was her ONLY son-in-law, but she loved saying it and he loved hearing it. Their relationship was incredibly special. He would have done anything for her to feel like a queen. When he got home every day and heard her special greeting for him, he would tell her, "Okay, okay, I'll get your drink" and we would all laugh. Of course, Rick and I would have to join in on the drinking, too,

My daughters had a special bond with mom. Monica experienced so much with her grandma because she was the first and only grandchild before Amanda was born and mom did not spoil either of the girls, but they did so much together. Monica remembers all the things they used to do. Amanda enjoyed her conversations with her grandma. In fact, they are similar in so many ways, especially when communicating with others. Both girls had a chance to reconnect with her in a way that they had not been able to due to frictions with my brothers. What family is not dysfunctional, right? So having mom live with us was a godsend. You see, our girls just live within a couple of miles from us, and we are right in the middle of their homes, with Monica to the north of us and Amanda to the south. They got to see mom frequently and we all loved it. We needed to make up for lost time.

Zander with Grandma Tillie

Her great grandchildren loved having their Granny here and that is an understatement. She had a knack for talking to the kids. They were always so receptive to her words of wisdom, which defied the norm. She would softly give them advice and they soaked it up. She constantly handed us pearls of wisdom and we use them to this day. Most had curse words, but some of the cleaner ones were:

- "To avoid arguments, listen to what people tell you, smile, nod and then do whatever the hell you please. In other words, just smile and not honey, smile and nod."
- "What other people say about you is none of your damn business."
- "Show me who your friends are, and I'll show you who you are."
- "Never stoop to a lower level. Be the bigger person."

Terry and Cyndie with Mom and I

Josie and Jeanne with Mom

After mom moved in with us, we told our extended family and friends that she had moved in with us and they were all welcome to visit her any time. After that was announced, the flood gates opened, and we had a revolving door with her countless friends, nieces, nephews, and cousins. Everyone came to spend time to get a hug from her, play games and even have a drink or two. Love and laughter constantly filled the house. Of course, she loved all the attention that was lavished upon her.

Amanda, Richard R., Sandra, Richard R. myself, Mom and Richard E.

In June, mom finally admitted she was getting old at 99½ years old. Not that she "was" old, but that she was "getting" old. I have her on video saying that and I still laugh when I see it. She never did admit to being old. She certainly was something else!

Six

Enjoying Outings

Gage with Grandma Tillie at Walmart

e would not let mom's inability to walk without a walker stop us from going out. We would take her shopping at all hours of the day and night. We would go to Walmart and let her use the electric scooter, and if the grand-kids went with us, oh my, that was a special treat. I have a video of her and the kids using light-sabers and fighting it out in the aisle of the toy section. That was truly a sight to see, and it leaves a smile on my face, thinking about it. Here is a snapshot of Gage playing with her.

Gigi sharing Jello with Grandma

If we did not cook at home, we would go out to eat, whether it was breakfast, lunch or dinner and she was always ready to get out of the house. Every so often, we would take her to Dairy Queen for a banana split. Of course, we would invite the kids and when they joined us, it was always a blast. Gigi loved sharing her desserts with her Grandma Tillie.

The Brownsville Cousins

When family members could not come to see mother, we would take her to visit them, regardless of where we had to drive. Mom was always ready for a road trip. Her saying was, "I've got my panties ready and packed!" We took her to New Braunfels, Corpus Christi, Comfort, San

Marcos, and even Brownsville to visit relatives who had not seen her in years, and it was so heartwarming to see her being loved by everyone we visited. It was beautiful.

Mom & Rick at the Kickapoo Casino with the Show Girls

In mom's older age, she could not go fishing, but her second favorite pastime was gambling. When she lived with my older brother and was still driving, she would go gambling every single day. And I am not talking about driving to Louisiana, I am talking about illegal gambling. She would tell us that she was going to "play the maquinitas." In English, that meant little machines, which was her way of saying that she was going out to play the slots. Even after she stopped driving, her girlfriend would pick her up almost daily. I would tell her, "Woman, I don't want to see you in the headlines of some newspaper, when they bust that illegal gambling place." She would laugh and say, "oh they won't catch me." While she was with us, we had to take her to the Kickapoo Casino, and she was so excited. That woman could last for hours, but we could not. Where did all that energy come from? Whew!

Seven

Tillie Turns 100 Years Young!

December rolled around quickly, and we all gathered at Monica's house for Christmas and to celebrate Moms' upcoming 100th birthday. This was the first time in a long time that both of our girls and all five grand-kids were under one roof and mom was super happy to have everyone together, especially at Christmas time. In fact, the picture here is my entire clan with mom. The first time that we had all our grandchildren in one room, with both girls. The only ones missing from this pic were Richard and Steven, Monica's husband as both were taking the pictures.

My brothers decided to throw mom a surprise party to celebrate her 100th birthday. Mom was going to be the belle of the ball and she had no clue.

Mom's Birthday Cake

In preparation of her surprise party, we gathered a list of friends and relatives. Although all of mom's brothers and sisters had passed years ago, she had a couple of first cousins who were younger and still alive, so we made sure to include them. We told her we were taking her to Corpus for a little gathering. She picked out a black dress with glitter of all colors and she loved it. Richard got us a couple of suites at a nearby hotel. We got her all primped up and she applied her own lipstick, which she always carried in her bag. She was always prepared.

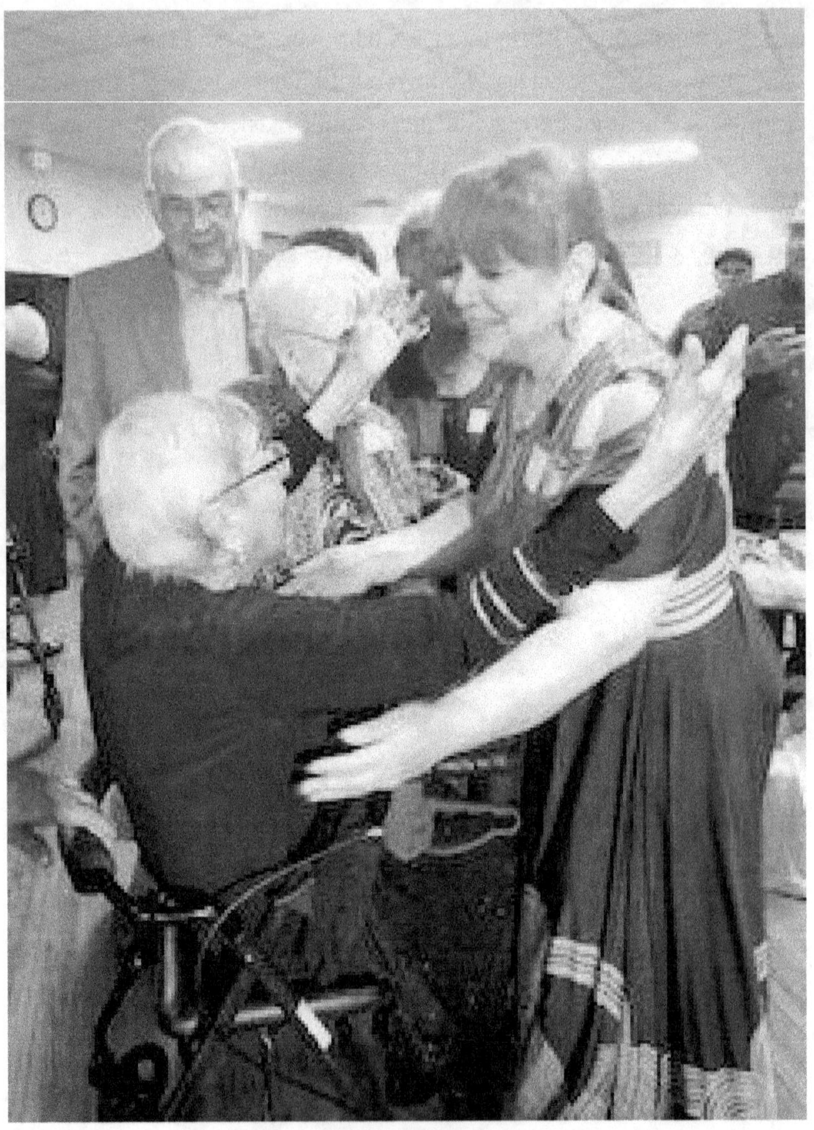

Everyone greets Mom at her party

We arrived at the event center and mom was shocked and pleasantly surprised to see everyone there. There must have been well over one hundred people, and she loved all the attention. Everyone was able to hug and visit with her and they all took pictures with her. We even took her out on the dance floor, with her walker of course and she loved every minute of it. We loaded all her gifts in Rick's car to bring them back home to San Antonio. That was a momentous day.

During our last day in Corpus, my other brothers invited mom and Rick for breakfast when they asked mom where she wanted to stay from now on. She said, "I want to go back home to Margaret's with Rick." I can only guess that thought she was not happy being with us. Mind you, none of my other brothers ever came to visit mom at our home before she passed away. They were always welcome, and I was not going to stop anyone from seeing her, like they did to me and my family. Regardless, right after breakfast, Rick happily brought mom home.

The following Monday after her party, mom started opening her gifts one at a time and she read every single card. She was so overwhelmed with all the love she received from everyone. I took pictures of her with most of the gifts, and there were a lot of them. I also called a few of the people so she could personally thank them.

SEXY SENIOR
CITIZEN

Eight

Covid 19 hits in 2020

As many of you know, in early 2020, Covid 19 hit the United States and we all went into quarantine. Mom loved it because I was laid off and was home every day, so I got to spoil her more than usual.

I then got a new job that allowed me to work from home. At times, mom forgot that I was working, and she would barge into my office. I eventually placed a sign on my office door, letting her know when I was working. Whenever I was not working, I would spend time with her. She wished I did not have to work, but it was only four days a week. During my free time, we would go out on the patio and work on her plants or enjoy a drink. Anything to get out of the house. One day, she asked Rick for a doobie and told him not to tell me. I just found that out during the writing of this book. Yes, my mom smoked a joint and I did not know. Dang mom!

During quarantine we visited and had Game Night with the family via Zoom

It was awful that we were unable to visit anyone or go anywhere. Fortunately, our daughters used the internet for us to get together virtually. We would have game nights on Zoom or use Face Time to visit, then I started face timing with anyone who had an iPhone. Mom got to see and talk to quite a few folks during that time, and I was so glad that we were able to do that. At the end of July, I was hospitalized with Covid and during the second week in the hospital, Rick called me to tell me that mom had a massive heart attack and passed away. WAIT, WHAT?!? This cannot be happening! How could that be?? I was devastated!

Nine

Moving on Without Her

Mom's funeral took place the day after I was released from the hospital, and I was unable to attend. I still cannot believe she is gone. I wish mom were still here, so I could talk to her.

Mom lived with us for 16 months prior to her passing, and I am very appreciative for the time we had with her. We expressed our love to her every single day and in more ways than we could count. Not a single day went by without telling her, "I love you," and she would tell me she loved me too, and I felt it. Our girls and grand-kids hugged her every chance they got. Andrew would come to visit and get his "Granny hug." In fact, Andrew and Gage are great huggers, just like mom. Their hugs are long, strong, and filled with love. So, in essence, she lives on in them.

Mom and I goofing off

Fortunately, my mother left us with many great memories that bring love and laughter to our days. She was so funny in her own way. From the time she woke up, to the time she went to bed, she had us laughing. Her nickname for me (and a lot of her friends) was, "Bartola." That is slang for chick or girlfriend. Gio, our youngest grandson, would laugh every time we said it. It was a funny word to him. Every night, she would tell me, "Good night, Bartola," and I'd kiss her good night and tell her, "I'll see you in the morning Bartola, I love you." Now, we use that term and fondly think of her with a smile. We are so fortunate to have so many pictures and videos of her shenanigans that will keep her memory alive for a long time to come. Even the grand-kids fondly remember the funny things she would say or do. They tell me how lucky they were to have had such a crazy great grandma. Few people can say that. I barely remember my grandma because she passed away when I was only four years old.

Mom doing what she does best!

Cheers!

Today, we could be having an alcoholic beverage and we will all say, "Cheers!" or "Hey Mr. Richard, I'll drink to that" and we just laugh remembering all the silly things she would say and do. My mother was a true gem.

Every so often, I find myself repeating something mom would say, and I think to myself, "like mother, like daughter." She is constantly in my thoughts, prayers, head and in my heart and I feel her with me. I do know she genuinely loved me. I find myself buying clothes with bright and beautiful colors, because I want to be like her. Family and friends have told me that I look like her. That is the ultimate compliment anyone can give me.

I often hear about people who had regrets when their parents passed away because of bad relationships they had. Luckily for me, I have absolutely no regrets or resentments. I was able to forgive my mom, and see past hurt, which enabled me to love her the way I wanted to be loved.

I do not expect anyone to understand how I grew to love mom, but I am glad that I was able to do it. I must admit, it is hard not having her with us, but I am moving on and living life to the fullest and in vivid color. After all, I had a great teacher!

Ten

Conclusion

Well, that is our love story, at least that is what I call it. I never really had the opportunity to grieve over mom's death. So, spending the time to write this book allowed me to be alone with my memories and thoughts and grieve over losing her. I absolutely loved writing this book in mom's honor, and I thank you for taking the time out of your busy day to read it.

If you enjoyed reading this book, I would be very appreciative if you would be so kind as to leave a favorable review for the book on Amazon.

Blessings to you and yours.

About the Author

Also by Margaret Mondragon